D1364793

FLORIDA

A Photographic Journey

TEXT: **Bill Harris**

CAPTIONS: **Pauline Graham**

PHOTOGRAPHY: **Werner J. Bertsch/Fotoconcept Inc.**
and Colour Library Books

DESIGNED BY: **Teddy Hartshorn**

EDITORIAL: **Gill Waugh and Pauline Graham**

PRODUCTION: **Ruth Arthur and David Proffit**

DIRECTOR OF PRODUCTION: **Gerald Hughes**

DIRECTOR OF PUBLISHING: **David Gibbon**

CLB 2457
© 1990 Colour Library Books Ltd., Godalming, Surrey, England.
© 1990 Illustrations: Werner J. Bertsch and Colour Library Books.
All rights reserved.
This 1996 edition is published by Crescent Books,
a division of Random House Value Publishing, Inc.,
40 Engelhard Avenue, Avenel, New Jersey 07001

Random House
New York • Toronto • London • Sydney • Auckland

Printed and bound in Malaysia

ISBN 0-517-01499-8

10 9 8 7 6

FLORIDA

A Photographic Journey

Text by
BILL HARRIS

CRESCENT BOOKS
NEW YORK • AVENEL, NEW JERSEY

In the history of the United States, almost no decade was more bizarre than the 1920s. A constitutional amendment had made alcohol illegal, and the entire country seems to have gone berserk.

Women were showing their knees in public for the first time. Men were wearing coonskin coats and sipping gin they made in their bathtubs from flasks they carried in their hip pockets. Law and order was personified by the Keystone Kops, and one of the heroes of the day was Al Capone. President Harding, who was said to have run the country from a "smoke-filled room," was at the center of a scandal over huge oil company bribes. Madness seemed to be everywhere, and even people who rejected the thrill-seeking life style of the Jazz Age got caught up in its enthusiasm at tub-thumping religious revival meetings.

If speak-easies and Chicago gangsters are the monuments of the '20s, Florida sunshine, bathing beauties and symbolic palm trees are its legacy. In a time when having a good time was all there was to do except make more money, Florida was the perfect place to do both.

Florida came to the attention of the rest of the country during the Spanish-American War in 1898. A great many servicemen were sent there for training and went back to live or vacation in Florida when the war was over. Even more Americans saw Florida for the first time in 1918, when they were sent there to learn to fly the planes in World War I. And by the time the age of the flapper was upon us, Florida was ripe for a boom.

It was the kind of hysteria the country hadn't seen since 1849, when gold was discovered in California. In this case, the gold was the land itself, but this time, people had cars to get them close to the mother lode, and slick advertisers had radio to let them know where to go. Hype was the word of the day, and the price of land in Florida, it seemed, had nowhere to go but up.

Just about everybody who lived in Florida played the real estate game in one way or another. And to people who drove down from up North in those days, the typical Floridian was a man in a white blazer and striped trousers, wearing a straw skimmer and leaning against the door of one of the thousands of real estate offices in Miami. The second most common Florida type was the "bathing beauty," and she was in the real estate business too. A pretty girl in a bathing suit was so common in Florida advertising that it's widely accepted today that the girls they call "bathing beauties" were invented there.

Before a hurricane ended the boom in 1926, more than seven billion dollars-worth of land was sold, and resold, in Florida. A lot of it was under water, but that didn't seem to matter to anybody, least of all the salesmen. People came in droves to "invest" their money. And why not? The ads told them that if they bought land, their trip to Florida would be paid for. In some cases, buyers were even offered a free car along with their lot. And anybody who just listened to a sales pitch was guaranteed at least a free lunch.

Florida was at the center of one of the biggest advertising blitzes of all time. And the hucksters trotted out the biggest names they could find to help get their message across. Gene Tunny, a contender for the heavyweight boxing championship in those days, was among the first, along with big league baseball stars. To lure bigger fish, the promoters hired the top golf professionals to compete in tournaments and casually discuss the merits of Florida as a heaven on earth for golfers. It was something of a coup because, at that time, only the rich played golf.

They didn't stop with sports figures, of course. William Jennings Bryan, who had been the U.S. Secretary of State and ran for president three times, made Coral Gables a base for his religious revival meetings, and helped sell a million dollars-worth of land a day at the same time.

If old-time religion didn't work, Evelyn Nesbit, the "girl on the red velvet swing" who was made famous the night Harry Thaw shot Stanford White in Madison Square Garden, joined other Broadway stars, like Ruby Keeler and Helen Morgan, in Florida nightclubs where the sales pitch became very hard to resist. One of the clubs was run by Texas Guinan, the owner of one of New York's most popular speak-easies. They loved her in Manhattan because she always began the evening's entertainment with a cheery "hello, suckers!" She loved Florida because, as she put it: "There can't be any suckers left on Broadway. They're all here!"

When sports, religion and wild parties didn't work, the promoters dipped into their bag of tricks and produced Feodor Chaliapin, the greatest opera star of his day, and Paul Whiteman to add another touch of class. And songs like *Moon Over Miami* were plugged all over the country to keep people tuned in to the fact that something was doing and Florida was doing it.

In Miami alone, there were 6,000 registered real-estate agents, and possibly even more press agents. They were selling a dream, and little else. Usually, they'd talk about a city that would be built some day somewhere the state. They'd show their eager customers a tract of land with nothing on it but a garish arch made of stucco that would, they said, be the entrance to a wonderful community. But the one they showed wasn't the tract they were selling. That was much better, of course, or so they said. Better still, the buyer could get in on "the ground floor" and make millions.

The boom didn't produce many real millionaires. A lot of people made that much on paper, but most of the speculators believed their own publicity and used their profits to buy more land, all the while driving up prices. By the time it ended, more than ninety percent of them had less money than when they started. The land was virtually worthless again, banks began to fail, construction stopped and grass began to grow on roads that had been built in anticipation of huge housing developments. Before the stock market crashed, in 1929, Florida was well into the Depression.

Not everyone lost, however. Some people resisted the urge to expand or sell out and weathered the storm very nicely.

Some, like David P. Davis, who bought two sand bars in Tampa and expanded them into the best residential neighborhood in the area, turned a nice profit. Carl G. Fisher invested in a swamp and turned it into Miami Beach. Henry Plant brought railroads and steamship lines to Florida, and Bion Barnett started a chain of safe banks through the influence he established with the state treasurer. The treasurer was afraid of Florida banks, and Barnett did him a favor by transferring his personal funds to a New York bank without charging him the usual fee of six dollars.

The real winner through it all was the State of Florida itself. During the boom, highways were built and, for the first time, roads went into the interior. Swamps had been drained and turned into rich farmland, bridges were built, canals dug and whole cities were established. The most important of them was Miami.

The boom centered on Miami, which before that had been a small town, indeed. One of the men who helped it grow was a Quaker from New Jersey named John S. Collins. When he arrived in Miami he was convinced it would become a major city, and he bought 1,600 acres of land across the bay, thinking it would become valuable as the site for a suburb. He had been a farmer up North, and so converted his acres to farmland. To make it easier to get the avocados he grew to market, he built a road along the edge of his farm and dug a canal through it. But he still needed boats to get his produce to the railroad across the bay. What he wanted was a bridge, and to get money for it, he approached Carl G. Fisher. In exchange for $50,000, Fisher got an interest in the bridge and 200 acres of land. He bought 260 more, and brought in dredges to pump sand into the swamps. Then he laid out streets and building lots and called it Miami Beach.

For years, Miami Beach was unchallenged as "America's Playground." The rich and famous flocked there, from Al Capone to Arthur Godfrey. And, even though Las Vegas, Hawaii and the Caribbean islands have siphoned off some of its business, the Beach still has a string of hotels that range from super-deluxe to "charming." It has 900 swimming pools, 400 tennis courts and 1,000 stores – from branches of Saks Fifth Avenue and Neiman Marcus to tacky souvenir stands. There are many Art Deco hotels and apartment buildings that have been placed on the National Register of Historic Places, making it a special preservation district. Many of them take advantage of their special status by putting on special "nostalgia nights," featuring '30s and '40s-style entertainment

Miami Beach has put a special stamp on the history of American architecture with the big resort hotels built there in the 1950s. Places like the Bal Harbor, Eden Roc, Doral and Americana Hotels are worth the trip just to see the ornate lobbies and public rooms that, in some circles, epitomize bad taste, but to others represent the most elegant surroundings in the country. One of them, the Fontainebleau, calls itself "The World's Greatest Hotel." It's ornate, it's gaudy, even outrageous. But, in a strange bow to taste of a different kind, it doesn't have a sign to identify it. Its original owner was pleased to tell anyone that it was "the world's most pretentious hotel," and he felt that if you couldn't find it, you probably couldn't afford it anyway.

The grounds are a formal Louis-XIV garden, and French antiques and statuary decorate the interior. When it was built, there were more employees than guest accommodations, guaranteeing everyone personal attention. Movie stars and presidents stayed there and superstars like Frank Sinatra entertained there.

When Jack Benny visited the hotel, he told reporters he thought it was beautiful. "But," he added, "they overdid things when they put a ten-piece orchestra in the men's room."

One of the lobbies, with an ocean view, has tropical greenery softening the effect of marble columns and crystal candelabra. It has three huge crystal chandeliers, marble floors and overstuffed armchairs set around glass coffee tables bearing huge bowls of fresh flowers. The rug is the color of money, as well it might be bearing in mind the cost of even off-season overnight accommodation.

The Fontainebleau's pool is so big it has an island with palm trees in the center and a five-story mountain alongside it, with four waterfalls and a slide, not to mention a bar and an aquarium. They call it "the most amazing pool between Cape Cod and Key West," and they're probably right. But if you don't care for it, there's always the beach just outside or another huge salt-water pool not far away.

The hotels are just one of the things that make Miami Beach unique. People-watching there is a sheer delight. The rich and super-rich are still regulars, just as they have been for fifty years. It's a treat to watch them sitting in the ornate hotel lobbies, dressed in gold lamé or the latest polyester ,with blue-colored hair and dour expressions, doing nothing but watching and being watched. More than half the people who live in Miami don't have fur stoles and Vuiton handbags. They're over sixty-five years old and live there on less a week than the daily cost of a hotel room. The contrasts are fascinating.

If Florida was the first to feel the effects of the Depression of the 1930s, it was also the first to come out of it. Miami never stopped expanding, and today "Greater Miami" covers more than 2,000 square miles. Part of the city itself is called "Little Havana," because it is home to more than a quarter of a million Cubans who moved to the United States after the Castro revolution. It isn't unusual to find stores in Miami with signs in the window saying, "English Spoken Here," and many Miami radio stations program only Latin music and broadcast in Spanish. The *Miami Herald* publishes an edition in Spanish as well as English. Thousands of businesses are owned and operated by the exiled Cubans, and just about everyone agrees they've added a very positive force to the area.

There's a bit of New York in Miami, too. Some of the best delicatessens south of New York's East Side are the pride of Miami. And many of the restaurants in town have been carefully planned to make New Yorkers feel right at home.

There was another Florida land boom in the 1960s but it may have been the quietest boom in history. Someone was quietly buying pine barrens in the middle of the state. The land wasn't worth much. It was under water part of the year, and considered unsuitable for anything but cattle ranching.

But these buyers weren't interested in cows, with the possible exception of one named "Clarabelle." They were representing a man from California named Walt Disney.

By the time Disney announced in 1965 that he was planning an East Coast version of Disneyland he had already bought 27,500 acres, an area twice the size of Manhattan, at an average cost of $185 an acre. Before the park opened in 1971, land nearby was selling for $300,000. It changed the lives of the local cowboys dramatically. Some of them sold out and retired. Others got on the bandwagon, opening motels, taco stands and shopping centers on just about every piece of available land within a 100-mile radius of Disney's "Magic Kingdom."

The Disney people anticipated that, and their "Vacation Kingdom" is surrounded by a natural buffer zone to give vacationers some relief from electric signs and jerry-built tourist attractions before they get to the main event.

Walt Disney World is quite possibly the world's greatest tourist attraction. It's certainly one of the world's most attractive, and so very carefully planned that if you don't have a good time there, you qualify as the world's greatest grouch.

They call the forty-three-acre core of Walt Disney World "The Magic Kingdom," and "magic" is a word that suits it very well. Even the people who work there are touched by it and have every bit as good a time as the people they serve.

There are two ways to get into the Kingdom; a futuristic monorail or a steamboat, either of which takes you to the Main Street Depot, gateway to special "lands," each with its own flavor. The theme of each is carried out in the landscaping and architecture and, most of all, in the "adventures" offered there. It takes a couple of days to sample all of them, and that's just part of the "world" Walt Disney has built.

The monorail takes guests right into the lobby of the fourteen-story Contemporary Hotel, where there is a panoramic view of the park from the roof. It's a special adventure at night when colored lights make Cinderella's Castle look especially enchanting, and boats on the huge man-made Lake Buena Vista chug around in a musical extravaganza they call the "Electrical Water Pageant." "Electrifying" is possibly a better word for it.

Within the Vacation Kingdom, you can go horseback riding or water-skiing, you can hike, play golf, have a picnic. You can stay overnight in a recreated Polynesian Village or the ultramodern Contemporary Hotel or camp out under the stars in the wilderness.

It's just a hop, skip and a jump from Walt Disney World to Cape Canaveral, where the space age began for America. In the middle of a wildlife preserve, the John F. Kennedy Space Center is the site of the launching pads that were used to send men to the moon.

And not far from it is the oldest city in the United States, St. Augustine, first built in 1565. It was a Spanish colony when it was built more than fifty years after Ponce de León discovered Florida on his way to look for the fountain of youth. Ponce de León never found the fountain, of course, though he was sure it was on the island of Bimini in the Bahamas. But he did find the Gulf Stream, a wide river of warm water from the Caribbean that runs past the Florida coast on its way across the Atlantic Ocean toward Europe. The Gulf Stream became the route for ships carrying gold to Spain from Mexico and Central America, and colonies like St. Augustine were established to help protect the ships.

It was the first European settlement in the United States, but as a fort it was a failure. Pirates took it over and sacked it twice. The British, eager to expand their American colonies, tried to take it over, too, but failed. Diplomacy won the day, and the Spanish ceded the colony to the British in 1763.

The British stayed there for twenty years, and they were eventful years for them, indeed. Way up north, their colonies were beginning to get restless and, before too long, they had a war on their hands. They called it a "revolution," the colonists said it was a war for "independence." Either way, a great many colonists wanted to stay British, and people who felt that way and lived in the Southern colonies went to St. Augustine for protection. And the British found the old Spanish fort, Castille de San Marcos, a very handy place to put people who didn't see things their way.

Because Florida stayed loyal to the British during the war, the colonists had a problem. England had four wars going at the same time: with its North American colonies, with France, with Holland and, most important to the Florida colony, with Spain. The Spanish had colonies in Louisiana, just to the west, and on the other side in the West Indies. But they managed to hold out in spite of it.

Then British diplomacy came into the picture again. When they ended the war with Spain in 1783, the English gave Florida back to the Spaniards in exchange for Bermuda. It made sense at the time. Florida was almost completely covered with thick jungles which made perfect hiding places for runaway slaves. The Indians were much less than friendly, and their twenty-year adventure in the Sunshine State had been very unrewarding. Bermuda, on the other hand, was wonderful for farming and there was no place for slaves to run to. They had originally exchanged Florida for Cuba and twenty-seven million dollars in captured Spanish treasure, so they felt they were way ahead of the game.

When the Spanish came back, the British settlers moved out. Within a few years, the only settlements worth mentioning on the whole peninsula were St. Augustine and Pensacola, and there wasn't much worth mentioning about them.

The U.S. Government bought it from Spain in 1821, and Florida was ripe for expansion once again. Just as they would 100 years later, Americans flocked to the new territory and began a chapter in American history most Americans would probably rather forget.

The Seminoles and Creeks were the two major Indian tribes in Florida at that time. And until that time they had been reasonably friendly neighbors. But the new settlers didn't travel all that distance to be neighborly. They didn't want to work too hard, either, and it was easier for them to take over Indian farms than to clear and drain their own. A lot of Indians were killed, more were driven off their land. But they didn't seem too eager to fight about it, preferring instead to retreat deeper into the recesses of the Everglades.

That wasn't enough for the new Floridians. They convinced the government that these savages ought to be on a reservation out West somewhere, where they couldn't "harm" anybody. It never occurred to any of them that "out West" was desert country, a far cry from the swamps these people had adapted to over generations.

But the Indians went along with the joke and sent a small delegation out to Oklahoma to have a look around. Most of them died there. But still the chiefs were anxious to make peace with the Great White Father and were set to sign their own deportation treaty when fate stepped in.

A gang of settlers, on a raiding party into the swamp, kidnapped a young Indian woman who was the wife of a Seminole named Osceola. Furious, he went to the white man's fort to protest. And he was thrown into prison for his trouble.

By the time he got out and back to the swamps, there was just one thing on Osceola's mind. Revenge. He became a powerful force among the chiefs and began to convince them the white man's treaty wasn't all they thought it was. By the time the chiefs assembled with the American military to sign the treaty, Osceola was the principal advisor to the most powerful of them.

When the Indians hesitated to sign the document, the American general began to threaten them. He said he would give orders to his men to shoot any Indian on sight as an outlaw. That was too much for Osceola. He leaped from his seat, pulled his knife from its sheath and plunged it into the treaty on the general's desk.

"This is the only treaty we will ever make with the white men!" he shouted.

And with that, the United States was officially at war with the Seminole Indians of Florida. It was a war that would last for seven years, would cost the United States more than 2,000 soldiers and twenty million dollars, not to mention the losses to civilians in terms of property, livestock, even their lives. On the other side, the Seminoles gave up fifty prisoners and twenty canoes, and really won the war. But before it ended, they lost Osceola.

The war had no sooner begun than Osceola appeared at the fort where he had been taken prisoner the day he went looking for his wife. He got his vengeance by killing the general in command as well as his aide.

Meanwhile, a troop of 110 soldiers, under Major Frances Dade, marched out from a fort in the Tampa area headed for Ocala to join an even larger force and then destroy the Seminole villages in the area. Had they succeeded, it would have been a glorious victory, with whole families of savages wiped out in the twinkling of an eye.

But instead of a "victory," the battle that took place is recorded in history as a "massacre." Dade's force was ambushed by Seminoles hiding in the dense woods. All Dade and his men could see were the flashes of their guns. And before they could return the fire, all but two of the company were dead.

It's since been estimated that there were never more than 1,000 armed Seminoles in all of Florida. The U.S. Army had 18,000 men stationed there. But the Indians had geography and determination on their side. The war dragged on for two years, and then Colonel Zachary Taylor arrived on the scene. "Old Rough And Ready," as they called this future President of the

United States, was able to wear them down, and even recommended removing some troops from Florida because the danger was apparently over. But "Old Rough And Ready" wasn't ready for Osceola.

Osceola convinced the chiefs they shouldn't surrender, and together they took 700 braves deeper into the Everglades.

The whites didn't know what to do next. The enemy had vanished. Their reaction was to raise an army of volunteers and go look for the Seminoles. But the Indians wanted peace, and so Osceola suddenly emerged from the swamp one day under a flag of truce.

He was clapped in irons and taken to St. Augustine. Later he was transferred, along with other prisoners, to Fort Moultrie, South Carolina. He was dead within a year.

His cause was taken up by another young brave, Coacoochee, the one they called "the wild cat." He was captured, along with other Seminoles, and put into prison. They all went on a hunger strike until they became thin enough to squeeze their bodies between the prison bars and escape. When they got back to their people, their people went on the warpath again.

For the next four years, Coacoochee and a small band of braves kept Northern Florida off balance in an almost constant state of terror. No one knew where they'd strike next. And they always struck furiously.

The war finally ended when he and a band of fifty Indians were captured at Fort Lauderdale. But the Seminoles have not signed a peace treaty with the United States to this day. The hatred is gone and the Seminoles know in their hearts they won the war. All they really wanted was to live in peace in the Everglades, and that's where you'll find most of them today. They still live the life of their ancestors, still practice the old tribal customs, still follow the ancient traditions. And they still remember Osceola, who even the whites now admit was one of the greatest warriors the Indian race has ever seen.

The Seminoles are one of the tourist attractions in the Everglades these days. But since the "glades" cover some 7,000 square miles, there's plenty of room for the few hundred surviving Indians and the several thousand tourists who go there to fish, to hike, to camp or to simply enjoy the incredible life that abounds in this mysterious setting.

The balance of nature is delicate in the Everglades. There are freshwater prairies and saltwater mangrove swamps, there are forests of cypress and forests of pine, there are coastal wetlands with saltwater marine life and vast glades of grass (which is where the name comes from) of more than 100 different varieties. There are thick jungles and wide open spaces. And most of it is below sea level.

Some parts of the Everglades have been reclaimed as farmland, and it's some of the richest farmland in the state. Huge yields of some thirty different kinds of vegetables help assure a year-round supply of fresh produce for the less fortunate Northern states.

But a major portion has become Everglades National Park, dedicated to guaranteeing survival for the huge variety of wildlife and plant life, even the land itself. A lot of the effort, as often happens, is a case of man protecting nature from man.

Nature had already provided a balance that, though delicate, was working very well when Ponce de León first pounced on the Sunshine State.

It's a balance that sometimes centers around the alligator, one of the original natives. They spend a lot of their time sticking their noses into the big holes that have been dissolved in the limestone that serves as a base for the Everglades. In the process, they clean out the holes which, during the long winter drought, act as natural basins for fresh water. The basins fill with fish and turtles and other tasty tid bits that keep the alligators supplied with food when there's too little water for them to get around. Birds and other animals feed on them too, and when the heavy rains start falling in May, the survivors run for their lives. When they get where they're going, they reproduce and provide more food for next winter.

Then one day, someone who thought he was smart and fashionable began making shoes and handbags, even watchbands, from alligator hide. And because most people will do anything if the price is right, alligator hunting became a game a lot of people played. Even though they get to be twelve-feet long and have jaws that can take a leg off before you can blink, the alligator is no match for a poacher. Before too long, alligators were on the endangered species list. Fortunately, sale of alligator hide is now illegal in the United States, and though markets, as well as the hunters who serve them, still exist, the good news for 'gators is that they are no longer "endangered," only "threatened."

There are crocodiles in the southern part of the Everglades, too. They have narrower snouts and lighter color, and a much more specialized habitat. At least as far as Florida is concerned, they are a very much endangered species because their habitat is vanishing before their eyes.

Alligators are the most popular attraction for Everglades visitors, but other unusual wildlife calls the area home, too. The manatee, for instance. These sea cows weigh almost a ton and grow up to fifteen-feet long, chewing on the plants growing along the sloughs. They don't have many enemies except the propellers of boats they occasionally come up to investigate.

Cougar, called Florida panther, stalk their prey in the pinewoods, and southern bald eagles nest in the trees. The birdlife of the Everglades is almost legendary, and a bird watcher hasn't seen anything until visiting there. There are spoonbills and pelicans, storks and herons, cranes, kites, hawks and falcons. The Everglades even has a special variety of cuckoo. Deer roam its woods, otter play in its waters, snapper and trout swim in its streams.

The Everglades is constantly changing. But as an attraction for visitors, it's a mysterious adventure that hasn't changed much since *The International Magazine* sent a correspondent there in 1898.

"The water in the Everglades is fresh and clear and sweet," he wrote. "We drank it and found it very good, barring the fact it was not cool. Alligators, white and blue herons, pelicans, fish hawks, water turkeys, turtles and many other creatures make this strange place their home. A lonelier, more uncanny region I cannot imagine. Yet there was a charm about it that will always keep it fresh in my memory.

"We saw all the regular sights to be found in the Everglades except the one we most wanted to see, viz. an alligator, and one within shooting distance...The nearest we came to seeing one was to hear him flop into the water just before we came into sight of the place where he had been.

"The fishing in the Everglades would meet the views of the laziest of men. The modus operandi is as follows: locate your boat right up against a luxuriant patch of lily pads, pull up one of these, tear open the stem, and nine times out of ten, you'll find as fat a little worm as any fish would wish. With this, bait a small hook and drop it over the side of your boat, and in a minute you'll have a minnow, which in turn goes on your bass hook, and there you are."

He didn't mention them, but when he visited there, huge flocks of flamingos competed with the sunsets. Some years ago, fashion decided their rosy-white feathers would make ladies much more beautiful. And that was the end of the flamingo flocks. There are still a few in the wild, but to see flamingos today, only parks, bird sanctuaries and Hialeah Race Track have enough to get an idea of what an exciting sight it must have been to find a flock of them at the edge of a lake.

The Florida Keys stretch out into the ocean below the Everglades. Its 106 miles from the mainland to Key West, and the highway that takes you there actually goes out over the ocean for one of the most unusual trips anywhere.

Ernest Hemingway loved the Keys because the fishing was fantastic. People who visit there today usually love it for the same reason. But there's another reason: the Florida Keys are incredibly beautiful to anyone who can't resist the pull of the sea. Actually, there are two seas to take your breath away on the way to Key West, the Atlantic on your left and the Gulf of Mexico on your right. And each has a personality of its own.

The word "Key" is left over from Florida's Spanish days when the dons referred to them as *cayos*, "little islands." Some of them are smaller than little. Some are big enough to contain whole towns. The highway that connects them was originally a railroad built in 1912. A hurricane destroyed it in 1935, and it was reborn as the road that exists today. At one point, the Overseas Highway stretches over a bridge seven miles long, an impossible piece of construction in 1912 but there it is!

There are tales of pirates every foot of the way between Key Largo and Key West. They say the floor of the ocean is covered with jewels and gold coins from Spanish galleons that were sunk in storms getting past the Keys. And they say the tiny islands made perfect hiding places for the likes of Blackbeard and Sir Henry Morgan. The stories are probably true and divers have no trouble finding plenty of evidence under that beautiful blue water. But the buried treasure is still buried. They say.

Big money came to the Keys in the boom days when people like Harvey Firestone and Henry Ford, Alfred DuPont and Herbert Hoover discovered Florida sunshine. After the sun, fishing was the big lure for these captains of industry looking for a little rest and relaxation. But to get proper rest, it's best to be among your own kind. So these gentlemen founded the very exclusive Anglers' Club at Key Largo. It was a tough club to join, so naturally a lot of people tried. When they were turned away, there were other people with less pride willing to take their money, and other clubs and resorts began to spring up nearby, so the Anglers' Club rejects could at least press their nose to the window and watch all those fabulous yachts put out to sea.

Little by little, expansion jumped from one key to the next and beachcombers who went there looking for bonefish and buried treasure swapped their simple life to help people keep up with the Firestones and Fords.

Then Humphrey Bogart and Lauren Bacall made a movie about Key Largo. President Harry Truman picked the Keys as his favourite vacation place. Hemingway had already made them as famous as Havana. And the Florida Keys became busy little islands.

But though it all, Key West hasn't changed a bit. It's been a thriving little city since the early part of the nineteenth century when it already had a small naval base, a thriving cigar factory, sponge fishing, treasure-hunting and the biggest population of any city in the whole state of Florida. It's a bit shabby, but that's part of its charm. It's a bit Old-World, and that's part of its charm, too. There are a lot of Cubans living there, making it a bilingual town much like Miami. But the Castro revolution wasn't their reason for going to Key West. It was the cigar business.

The houses still have their original charm, but they're a little dowdy by any other town's standards. The streets are alive with flowers, the docks alive with the sounds and the smells of the sea. The saloons are just as exciting as they were in Hemingway's day, and the girls are just as pretty, the cafés just as lively. And the birds in the trees are just as beautiful as when John Audubon decided Key West was a perfect place to live.

There simply isn't another town in the country that's quite like Key West. And the automobile trip that gets you there makes it even better.

Most Florida chauvinists agree their state is heaven on earth, but they disagree about whether it's at its best on the Atlantic Coast to the east or the Gulf Coast to the west. The subject rarely comes up in Key West because it's on both. But as you go farther north, you hear the argument over evening cocktails almost as much as you hear talk of Florida sunshine.

The East Coast has Miami, of course, and Daytona Beach, once used as an automobile speedway. Why, back in '03, Alexander Winton got his car up to sixty-eight miles an hour on the hard sand of Daytona. That's more than a mile a minute, and was pretty exciting stuff..not to mention a world record...back then. A lot of much faster records have been set in the years since, and the Daytona "500," at the speedway there, is one of the world's major car racing events. Ordinary folks drive their cars on the beach these days but the records they set are at the other end of the scale, thanks to the beach's ten-mile-an-hour speed limit.

Florida's Atlantic coast has Palm Beach too. Even people who consider Florida *declassé* sit up and take notice when Palm Beach is mentioned. Some of the best, and most expensive, hotels on the entire Atlantic Coast have made this a millionaire's playground since it was established at the turn of the century as "the Newport of the South." It was designed as a non-commercial, formally landscaped community (the business center was across Lake Worth in West Palm Beach) with expensive mansions, no cars and all the charm money could buy.

The original settlers were Vanderbilts and Whitneys, Roosevelts, Winthrops and Phippses. The tax rolls in the 1890s could easily have substituted for the Social Register. Their descendants still go there and, for them, it hasn't changed much. It's a favorite hunting ground for girls looking for rich husbands, and it isn't unusual to see seventy-year-old men in Gucci loafers with pretty young women who are obviously not their granddaughters.

In recent years it's become possible for ordinary wage slaves to enjoy Palm Beach. People who can't afford a room at the elegant old Breakers Hotel can find Howard Johnson's or the Holiday Inn not far away.

The East Coast is livelier. It has more hotels, more restaurants, more discos. It has dog tracks and jai-alai. And although there are more people on the beaches, they wear less, and that's an attraction, too.

At its widest point, Florida is only 361 miles across, but to many people, the two coasts are a world apart. There's more room on the Gulf Coast, actually about double the amount of shoreline, and the pace is generally slower.

If was a favourite with pirates back at the turn of the eighteenth century when treasure ships sailed the Spanish Main. The coast is laced with coves and inlets that made finding the swashbucklers just about impossible. Besides, as anyone who's there now will tell you, it's a nice place to live.

Pirates are a colorful lot, but the most colorful of them all, José Gaspar, the man they called "Gasparilla," gives Tampa one of its most fascinating attractions. Once a year, they have a five-day, Mardi gras-like celebration that ends with Gasparilla and his cutthroats taking the city by storm.

José Gaspar began life as the son of a Spanish nobleman, in 1756. He grew up with the best of everything: a fine education, the best clothes, and aristocratic surroundings. When he joined the Spanish Navy, it was generally agreed he would become one of its best admirals. He had good looks, good breeding, good backing and a very promising future.

But one thing was wrong. José Gaspar was a thief.

He made the rank of captain, and was so well trusted that he was given the assignment of delivering some of the king's most precious jewels. But when the package was opened, it was discovered that José had helped himself to some of them. And he himself was nowhere to be found.

Naturally, he didn't want to go to prison over a few baubles, so he stole a ship. It was said he was so charming, the crew of the ship was won over instantly, and even cheered when he hauled down the Spanish flag and hoisted the black flag of a pirate.

He sailed for the Spanish Main and found a perfect hiding place in Charlotte Harbor on the Southwest Florida coast. He set up shop on a little island there. He built a fort to protect it and a palatial house so he could live in the style he enjoyed. Then he changed his name to Gasparilla and proclaimed to one and all that he was "king of the pirates."

He was known all over the Gulf as a desperado of the first order. Merchantmen sailing out of New Orleans were terrified of him. Even the other pirates steered a wide path around him. He was a dead shot with a pistol, an expert rifleman, could handle a sword better than anyone on the coast, and his skill with a long gun was legendary.

Whenever he boarded a ship, he made it a point never to kill any of the women aboard. He was a gentleman, after all. But courtly manners had nothing to do with the custom. He had a harem on his little island. The ladies lived there in grand luxury, surrounded by the loot of thousands of luckless ships. When he tired of a woman, he'd give her to one of the members of his crew. That was one of the reasons why his crew kept growing, and why other pirates threw in their lot with him. But it was just one of the reasons. The crews of the ships he captured were given a choice of a pirate's life or death. And Gasparilla didn't find murder, even for small offenses, difficult at all

Naturally, the countries whose ships he was destroying fought back. And after a few years of having the Gulf all to himself, Gasparilla realized his days as a pirate were numbered. He divided his treasure among his men, took some favorites from his harem and sailed off in search of a safer lair. He had, in effect, retired. But he wasn't a retiring sort. As he was sailing out of the bay, a British merchantman came into view. In a parting shot, Gasparilla decided to take her.

But before he could fire a gun, the merchantman hoisted an American flag and fired a broadside from a battery of hidden guns. Their shots were true and the pirate ship became a mass of twisted rigging and dying men. They had him.

Of all the words that have been used to describe the king of the pirates, "proud" is probably the one that suits him best. At this moment, it was apparent that he had lost everything. But not his pride. He grabbed a piece of cable chain and wrapped it around his waist. Then, in a final gesture of defiance, he leaped overboard and was never seen again.

The Lafitte brothers, Billy Bowlegs, Sir Henry Morgan and hundreds of others were the scourge of the Gulf during the seventeenth, eighteenth and nineteenth centuries, but the British and American pirate chasers finally put them out of business. The only pirates who go there today are the Pittsburgh Pirates, one of the seventeen major league baseball teams that go to Florida's West Coast every year for spring training.

They go there because the climate is so wonderful. Back in 1885, the American Medical Association said that St. Petersburg was the healthiest place in America. According to the Chamber of Commerce, the sun shines 361 days a year. Because of it, the area has become one of the most popular retirement centers in a state where being retired or serving the retired is a major industry. There are young people there too, of course. It's the site of an annual invasion by college students on spring vacations, and the Chamber of Commerce swears the average resident is twenty years old.

There are some people who don't agree with that. S.J.

Perelman, the humorist, went there a short time ago to visit his old friend Lillian Hellman. When he got back, he told *The New York Times*, "I don't think I met a real Floridian or heard a single Florida idiom except 'come back and see us real soon.'... There are an awful lot of retirement villages and mobile-home villages, which lends no end of character to the general air of eyesore.

"... All that the inhabitants seem to do is walk up and down in front of shops selling women's wear marked down. This vast crowd of people – usually composed of two elderly ladies – circulates turgidly, staring numbly at the windows. Everybody comes down to Florida numb or has numbness thrust upon him."

He finished the interview by saying he was dying to see it all again. "I'm training a team of wild horses to take me back," he said.

Well, that's Perelman's opinion, of course. Actually, St. Petersburg is more youthful than it was twenty years ago. Back then, it was famous for its "green benches," which were placed along the main streets at convenient intervals for the elderly. But the benches are gone now and the average age has dropped considerably.

Children of all ages find fun in Sarasota and nearby Venice, the winter home of Ringling Brothers, Barnum & Bailey Circus. The "Greatest Show on Earth" gets its act together in Venice each year. And circus buffs get a year-round treat at the Ringling Circus Museum and the Circus Hall of Fame at Sarasota.

John Ringling took his circus to Sarasota in the 1920s and made it his own permanent home. The house he built is a copy of the Doge's Palace in Venice, and is one of the greatest houses in the United States. He was a collector of Baroque art, and his collection, one of the most important in the country, is the centerpiece of the museum he built. It has the largest collection of the work of Peter Paul Rubens outside Europe, along with priceless tapestries and the paintings of other masters of the period. The house is something of a museum itself, with gold-plated bathroom fixtures, a massive pipe organ and a marble terrace leading to the water's edge.

The house and museum are complemented by an eighteenth-century theater brought stone by stone from a small town near Venice. It's Florida's official state theater, used for operas and plays all year round.

There's another famous house farther south in Meyers. Thomas Edison worked there at the turn of the century, and the museum that was his home is crammed with his nearly 2,000 inventions, from the curling iron to the phonograph and the motion picture machine.

Without his movie machine, the outside world may never have discovered cowboys and Indians. They have both in Florida, but in this case, some of the cowboys are Indians. The biggest cattle ranches in the East are in Central Florida, and some are owned by descendants of the Seminole.

If cattle ranching in Florida seems to defy an American tradition, consider the fact that they also grow oranges and grapefruit in Texas. But oranges found their way to the United States through the Spaniards, who came to Florida more than four centuries ago. They were something of a luxury until after the Civil War, and up until that time not many people in the North, and even some Floridians, had ever seen an orange, much less tasted one. Oranges were shipped to New York and Boston from North Africa, which is on the same latitude as Florida, as novelties for children's Christmas stockings. But only the rich could afford them, and the Florida oranges were generally eaten by the people who grew them and no one else.

After the war they began shipping then, but the growers were an independent lot, each producing a different variety and competing for distribution. It only served to confuse consumers, and it could hardly be called an "industry."

They were growing grapefruit and limes by then too. But all the advertising genius available was selling land, and no one in Florida was bothering to tell the rest of country that citrus fruit was good for your health and great for your palate.

Then the California growers got into the act.

The Californians offered a thicker-skinned orange – not as juicy, not as sweet. But it had the advantage of better color – Florida varieties are often tinged with green – which made them look prettier, even though they weren't as well suited to American taste.

The Californians also had organization, promotion, efficient distribution and determination. By the 1920s they had flooded the market with orange juice and, even though most Americans preferred oranges from Florida, they were buying the West Coast competition.

By 1935 the Florida growers had finally got the message. They formed cooperatives, set standards and started advertising. In spite of it, they were still out in the cold and the Californians were as serious a threat as a hard frost in December. They also had to face the problem that theirs was a seasonal crop and, at the peak of the season, over supply makes it an unprofitable one, but in the face of the problems was a solution. Instead of dumping crops, they began canning them.

It started with grapefruit sections and eventually led to frozen concentrated orange juice. It made citrus products available all year round, and Florida started telling the rest of the country that "a day without orange juice is like a day without sunshine." California is still a factor in the citrus business, of course, but Florida keeps them hustling.

Florida's orange and grapefruit groves are centered in the Lake District of inland Florida. It's also the place where water-skiing was invented, at Cypress Gardens; where sports-car racing is a fine art, at Sebring; where scuba diving is a beautiful adventure, at Silver Springs.

Some of the Old South still lives in the Lake District, though an old native-born Georgian would probably laugh at the suggestion. Though Florida's population consists largely of transplanted Northerners, the original migrants from other states moved down from Georgia. Poor white people all over the South in the eighteenth century were known to their neighbors as "crackers." Farther North, the same people would have been called "hillbillies." The name seems to have come from their practice of carrying long bull whips for no other apparent reason than making a lot of noise.

When they took their collards and cowpeas, mustard greens

and white bacon farther south, the name went with them and eventually applied only to Floridians. Their relatives in the other Southern States became known as "rednecks."

As a testament to the hard sell that built Florida, the name "cracker" was used in the nineteenth century for anybody in the country "given to excessive boasting."

One of the people who popularized the romance of the Old South was a songwriter named Stephen Foster. He obviously loved the South and knew it well, but apparently he never saw the place in Florida that is still a symbol of everything Southern, the Suwannee River. There's a story that says his original draft of the song *Way Down Upon The Swannee River* had the name "Pedee River." In a lucky stroke of genius he changed it, after studying a map in search of a river with a two-syllable name. It was a map with a typographical error, apparently.

He couldn't have picked a more beautiful place to write about. The river's banks are lined with oak trees decked out in Spanish moss, and cotton fields stretch away from it into the distance. Watermelons, tobacco and peanuts complete the picture. Romance abounds there, too. In just about every part of the country where there's a cliff overlooking a river, the locals call it "lover's leap." The Suwannee has one, too. The legend is that a beautiful Indian maiden, distraught over the death of Osceola, ended her life by jumping over the side.

"In Florida has always been a place for lovers ... lovers of life and beauty. It's the Deep South with a difference. Back in 1888, *The New England Magazine* reported:

"In Florida the rest of the country has found its Persian gardens and its parks and waters where the winter does not come. Across its territory the breezes of the Gulf and the Atlantic are always at play. Bays and inlets that invite hospitality from the sea indent its shelly coast. Its territory is watered by fine navigable rivers, begemmed with lakes and ponds, laced with the clearest brooks, and all are fed from the most marvellous springs, many of them possessing medicinal virtues. The forests that darken the land are of genuine magnificence. Live oaks, pines, cedars, cypresses, magnolias and other flowering trees keep it verdurous from the beginning to the end of the year, and load the atmosphere continually with their healing and invigorating balm ... It is a land running over with abundance."

It wasn't possible to envisage what Florida would become back in 1888, and while the hand of man has changed it, the hand of nature is still as steady after nearly a century.

It's still a land of opportunity as much as it is a land of sunshine. It's as wonderful a place to live as it is to visit. Ask any cracker.

Tallahassee, Apalachee Indian for "Old Fields,"
is the capital of Florida. Its gracious, neoclassical
Old State Capitol building (previous page),
completed by 1845, when Florida became a state,
has been restored to its turn-of-the-century
condition. Its function as Capitol was transferred
later to the new twenty-two-story building which
overlooks it. Jacksonville (right), now one of
Florida's largest cities, was once just a cattle ford
on the St. Johns River. Indeed, while under
British rule the town was called Cowford. Later,
of course, it was renamed for Andrew Jackson.

Despite the fact that Jacksonville's St. Johns River is lined with modern skyscrapers and is the commercial center of the region, the city contains many beautiful old houses. One lovely example is mellow, Mediterranean-style Epping Forest (above), built in Jacksonville for Alfred I duPont. Top left: a prairie style house on Riverside Avenue, Jacksonville. Kingsley Plantation (left), on Fort George Island, near Jacksonville, is believed to be the oldest plantation house in Florida. The island was given to John McQueen in 1791 by the king of Spain. Eventually it passed into the hands of Zephaniah Kingsley, an ingenious slave broker, for whom it is named. Besides training the imported slaves in plantation techniques before selling them, he added oranges to the plantation's produce. He actually married the daughter of an African East Coast king and she, Anna Madegigine Jai, oversaw the slave training – at the same time keeping in check her husband's eye for other women in the slave cargo. The "widow's walk" on the top of the building was used as a platform from which to extinguish roof fires.

On St. Augustine's day, April 2, 1513, Juan Ponce de León – a Spanish explorer in search of the fountain of youth – put ashore on a new coast. It was the time of Pascua Florida, the Easter festival of flowers in Spain, and the land "having many pleasant groves," Ponce de León named it Florida. It is probable that the longest recorded history of any of America's fifty states began in St. Augustine, thought to be the place where Ponce de León landed. A great deal of this history involved territorial disputes between the Spanish, British, French Huguenots, Indians and Americans, and many of the consequent fortifications survive. Castillo de San Marco (above and right), in St. Augustine city, St. Johns County, is North America's oldest masonry fort. It was begun by the Spanish in 1672, built of native coqina, and took twenty-five years to complete. Fort Clinch (top right), named for General Duncan Lamont Clinch, was begun in 1847, too late for the preceding Spanish conflicts and not soon enough to be ready in time for the Civil War.

Above: the Bridge of Lions in St. Augustine. Marineland (facing page) lies on the ocean between St. Augustine and Daytona Beach, and offers shows and underwater exhibits demonstrating the riches of the Atlantic, including displays by performing dolphins.

The first world speed record set at Daytona Beach (these pages) was sixty-eight miles per hour and was achieved by Alexander Winton in 1903. Daytona has three beaches: one on the Atlantic coast and one on each side of the Halifax River. Its Atlantic beach consists of twenty-three miles of densely packed white sand, 500 feet wide and ideal for speed racing. Now, however, speed racing takes place at the Daytona International Speedway. Motor vehicles are still allowed on the beach at low tide, but they are regulated by a strict speed limit. Daytona's motoring prominence attracted such names as William Vanderbilt, John Jacob Astor and Henry Flagler to the area, but Daytona offers just as much to those visitors who are not racing enthusiasts. Watersports, for example, are available all year round, the October and November surfing championships attracting people from all over the world.

The Federal government's purchase of more than 88,000 acres of land near Merritt Island in Brevard County, Cape Canaveral, marked the beginning of the John F. Kennedy Space Center. The first Canaveral launch in 1950 established this part of Florida as home to the most sophisticated of America's aerospace technology. Its most famous recent development is, of course, the Space Shuttle.

The skyline of Orlando is that of a modern, thriving city, expanding due to its proximity to Disney World, Kennedy Space Center and Cape Canaveral. Originally a center of citriculture, Orlando was first settled in 1835 after the Seminole Wars. The site was chosen because of its nearness to Fort Gatlin, and was probably named after Orlando Reeves, a runner between Mellonville and Fort Gatlin, who was killed by Indians on the site of the town.

In Walt Disney World (these pages) fantasy is reality, and there can be no more fitting symbol of Disney World than Cinderella Castle (facing page), whose architectural inspiration was drawn from twelfth- and thirteenth-century France, where Charles Perrault's classic fairytale originated, and the mad Bavarian King Ludwig's castle at Neuschwanstein. Above: the Epcot Center, described by Walt Disney as "a showcase to the world for the ingenuity and imagination of American free enterprise."

Cypress Gardens (these pages and overleaf) were created in Central Florida in 1936 and today consist of 228 acres of botanical gardens and family theme areas. With their display garden alw● in bloom, Cypress Gardens are a potent reminder of why Ponce de León named the area Florida. Mr. Dick Pope, who created Cypress Gardens, was a pioneer of watersports, and waterski show● and watersports are major features of the gardens. Overleaf: the evening sun outlining the tall cypress trees from which the gardens take their name.

Cigar-making, phosphate-mining, tourism and commercial fishing have all contributed to making Tampa, Hillsborough County, the thriving and modern town it is today. However, it also retains much of its Latin ambiance, attesting to its Spanish origins. The area was probably first explored by a European in 1528 when Panfilo de Narvaez set foot there. He was followed by Hernando de Soto in 1539. However, local Indians warded off any permanent settlers until the Americans established Fort Brooke in 1824. Today, it is difficult to imagine Spanish explorers and Indian wars in Florida's leading industrial city.

43

Tarpon Springs (these pages), named for one sea creature, actually became famous for another. Greek sponge fishermen moved here from Key West, bringing with them their culture, cuisine and neo-Byzantine architecture. The town is still Greek in character and still one of the world's largest sponge markets. The Spongeorama (facing page) is a complex offering dioramas, films and a spongers' village, all depicting the history of the sponge industry.

Moored in St. Petersburg's Vinoy Basin, MGM's version of The Bounty *lies fully and authentically outfitted, serving as a museum of marine life. On shore is a replica of the longboat in which Captain Bligh and his eighteen loyal crew members were set adrift and made their unbelievable 3,600-mile journey to shore after the mutiny. Appropriately, the gift shop sells examples of the disappearing art of skrimshaw from Pitcairn Island, made by descendants of the mutineers who settled there. Overleaf: Clearwater at night.*

Above: Sarasota Jungle Gardens. Also found in Sarasota is the ornate Venetian mansion built in 1925 by John Ringling in imitation of the doges' opulence. Ca'd'Zan (overleaf), or "house of John" in the Venetian dialect, is a treasure house of marble floors, gold fittings, chandeliers, ornate windows and architectural extravagance. In the grounds of Ca'd'Zan stands the John and Mable Ringling Museum of Art (facing page), built in the Italian Renaissance style and housing, among the work of other European artists of the baroque era, paintings by Rubens.

Vanderbilt Beach on Florida's west coast. Also on the west coast, off Fort Myers where Thomas Edison had his winter home, lies the island of Captiva (overleaf). This was a favorite retreat of President Theodore Roosevelt, who went there for the deep-sea fishing, and watersport enthusiasts still flock to the beaches to sail and surf. The beaches of Captiva are particularly noted for the number and variety of their shells: over 300 kinds have been recorded, including multi-colored calico shells.

Naples (these pages), the county seat and principal city of Collier County, is a relatively new city. It had about 1,500 residents in 1950 but, in 1960, Hurricane Donna swept away much of the town. The area has been a noted resort since 1887, billed as a place "where roses bloom in December ... and surf bathing is enjoyed in January." Its seven-mile-long beach (overleaf), washed by the waters of the Gulf, is a major attraction, as are the Venetia Island shopping (above) and residential (right) areas.

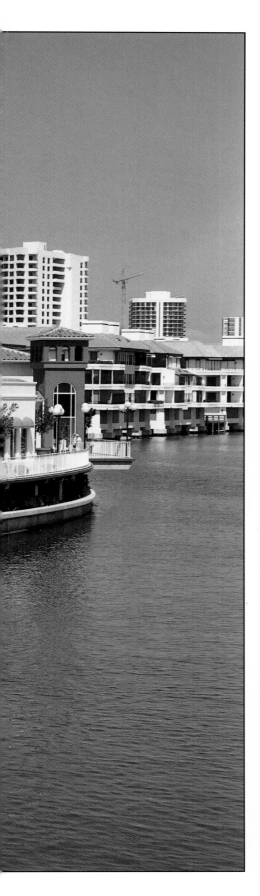

Jenson Beach (facing page), on Florida's Atlantic coast, lies on a sliver of land between the St. Lucie Inlet and the Indian River, providing a convenient yacht basin that can handle craft up to 120 feet long. Directly east of Jenson Beach lies Hutchinson Island (above). This island's most famous beach visitors are not its tourists, but the loggerhead sea turtles which come ashore to lay their eggs during the summer months.

The House of Refuge at Gilbert's Bar Inlet,
Hutchinson Island, dates from 1876 and was
built to accommodate shipwreck victims thrown
ashore from vessels broken up by the Atlantic.
During the nineteenth century, ten such houses
of refuge were built on Florida's east coast.
Stuart (overleaf) is known as the "Sailfish
Capital of the World." A famous water chase
from the Bond film Moonraker was filmed in
Stuart on the St. Lucie River.

Hobe Sound Beach lies on a stretch of coast best known for the Hobe Sound National Wildlife Refuge, which affords protection to nesting turtles. Overleaf: a yacht harbor in Port Salerno on the St. Lucie Inlet.

In 1888, when Henry Flagler's railroad opened up the Gold Coast, the line served southeast Florida and was referred to locally as the "Celestial Railroad" because, in those days, its four stops were Jupiter, Mars, Venus and Juno. The Jupiter lighthouse (facing page), built in 1860, is one of the oldest mainland lighthouses on Florida's Atlantic coast. The beach (above) on Jupiter Island affords excellent conditions for windsurfing. It hosted its first international surfing competition in 1983.

The beach at Lake Worth is a popular tourist attraction, luring many sun seekers to the town which lies south of Palm Beach on Florida's east coast.

Above: Lantana Beach, south of Lake Worth. Boca Raton (right), in Palm Beach country, lies about fifteen miles north of Fort Lauderdale. Its name comes from the Spanish phrase bocca rattones, *meaning "mouth of the rat," which refers to the sharp, incisor-like rocks offshore, like rodent's teeth gnawing away at ships' cables. Its tranquil-looking beach belies the implied danger of its name. Overleaf: the elegant Breakers Hotel, Palm Beach, showing Moorish and Spanish influences in its architecture. If Palm Beach looks a little like Italy's Portofino, it is probably through the work of architect Addison Mizner, who arrived in Palm Beach in 1918 and designed a great many Mediterranean-style buildings decorated with Italian-style tileware.*

Pompano Beach, Broward County, lies between Miami and Palm Beach. Besides being a major tourist resort, it is a notable sporting center. The Texas Rangers carry out their spring training here, and it is also the training center for the Fort Lauderdale Baseball School. Moreover, the Pompano Park Harness Raceway is the number one harness track in Florida.

Pompano Beach (left) is famous for its unusual horse farm, which boasts a collection of forty-eight performing miniature thoroughbreds and offers children the chance to see seventeen- to thirty-one-inch-tall Arabians and Clydesdales. Deerfield Beach (above), on Deerfield Island, is part of Deerfield Island Park, a haven for the many species of birds that live in the Intracoastal Waterway. Deerfield Island was also notorious as the place where Al Capone, Chicago's most famous gangster, once hid out. Overleaf: Johnston Street, Hollywood.

As early as 1450 B.C., aboriginal Tequesta Indians roamed the New River area (overleaf) of Fort Lauderdale (above), and it is believed that Juan Ponce de León explored the area around 1513, in quest of the fountain of eternal youth. In 1837, Major William Lauderdale led his group of Tennessee Volunteers to build a stockade on the banks of the New River to fend off attacking Indians during the Seminole wars, and so began Fort Lauderdale. Artificial islands were added in the 1920s and now the city boasts 165 miles of lagoons, canals and rivers – earning it the title "Venice of America." Facing page: Hollywood beach.

Miami Beach (right and overleaf), thriving and modern, was marked on sixteenth-century Spanish maps as a Tequesta Indian village. Its Indian name, Mayaimi, probably means either "big" or "sweet water" — both of which are still appropriate to modern Miami.

At the Bayside Shopping Center (facing page and overleaf) in downtown Miami, tall buildings, such as the Centrust Tower (above) rise above dwarfed palm trees and moored boats. Miami has developed very rapidly since the days when Julia Tuttle settled there to raise citrus fruits in a frost-free environment in 1890.

Miami's Coconut Grove boasts a tranquil yacht harbor which seems especially serene alongside commercial Miami. Overleaf: the Port of Miami.

99

Work on Villa Vizcaya (these pages) began in 1914 and, during the two years of its construction, as many as 1,000 craftspeople worked on what is now claimed to be America's finest example of the Italian Renaissance Revival style. Its architects, Burrall Hoffman Jr. and Paul Chalfin, augmented this style with some individual touches of their own, stuccoed the exterior with a coral trim and shipped in pieces from genuine Italian palaces. The front (above), overlooking Biscayne Bay, is characterized by a galleon-shaped, stone terrace, while at the rear (right) lie several acres of stepped gardens. James Deering, the co-founder of International Harvester, had it built and lived there until his death in 1925. This seventy-room Venetian villa is now the Dade County Art Museum and still houses many of the treasures Deering himself collected.

Long ago flamingos were a great deal commoner in Florida than they are today. Nonetheless, around Flamingo Lake (left) in Miami's Parrot Jungle (these pages) they can still cluster as they would have done in the wild. Approximately 2,000 varieties of plants grow in Parrot Jungle, and 1,000 birds fly freely.

Miami's Seaquarium covers sixty acres beside Biscayne Bay and is home to 10,000 marine animals. It was designed to be both entertaining and educational, and features many performing creatures, including killer whales. Viewing tanks enable visitors to study a variety of sealife at close quarters.

The Cypress Mangrove Swamp (facing page) in Florida's Everglades National Park (these pages) is a reminder of the wilderness that once enveloped the area. The Everglades provided the last refuge of Osceola's band of rebel Indians, who had eventually balked at the white man's 1823 treaty relocating Indians in order to accommodate settlers. Their descendants still live in this national park. Above: alligators sunning themselves in the Everglades.

Left: Islamorada on Upper Matecumbe Key. This Key is said to have taken its name from a corruption of the Spanish *mata hombre*, "kill man," which is also the translation of *Cuchiyago* – the Indian name for the island. The word *key* is a corruption of the Spanish *cayo*, meaning small island, and some of the island's Spanish history is close at hand: the wreck of a Spanish galleon lies just offshore. Below: Key Largo, the nearest to the mainland and the longest of the keys.

Just off Islamorada (facing page and overleaf) lies the Theater of the Sea (above), an outdoor sea aquarium which has the prestige of being America's second oldest such attraction. Marine shows, in which dolphins dive in and through bottomless boats, are staged in its natural lagoon. Overleaf: Islamorada's Plantation Yacht Club bathed in evening color. Islamorada was named from the Spanish for island, isla, and purple, morada, the Spanish probably having encountered one of the occasional drifts of the violet-colored sea snail Janthina janthina offshore.

If, as Don Marquis said, fishing ever was "a delusion entirely surrounded by liars in old clothes" in the Florida Keys, it is so no more. The fishermen around Faro Blanco marine resort (right) on Marathon Key clothe themselves in elegant and expensive boats.

The further south one gets in the Florida Keys, the more space there is for camping and other kinds of outdoor pursuit – especially in Bahia Honda State Park on Bahia Honda Key (left), where eighty acres are available for campers and picnickers to explore.

The natural beauty of the Florida Keys (overleaf) is spanned by a man-made wonder, the Seven Mile Bridge (these pages), which runs from Knight's Key to Pacet Key and is the longest segmental structure in the world.

The southernmost city in the continental United States, Key West (these pages and overleaf) has attracted many famous characters to its relaxed way of life. President Harry Truman, for example, had a winter home in Key West. Perhaps the most famous, or infamous, of them all was Ernest Hemingway. Tennessee Williams, another of America's most prominent writers, lived here too. The Lighthouse Museum (left) stands on Whitehead Street, where both Ernest Hemingway and John James Audubon once lived. Duval Street (above) boasts the oldest house in Key West, a sea captain's house dating from 1829, with a characteristic "landlubber's tilt" and a ship's hatch in the roof. Following page: sunset at Whale Harbor.

INDEX